The Power to BECOME

Mattie Stanford Johnson

UALLo.w.e.d Publishing

Chicago, IL

Copyright © 2017 by **Mattie Stanford Johnson**

All rights reserved. No part of this publication may be reproduced, distributed or transmitted in any form or by any means, without prior written permission.

Mattie S. Johnson/Publishing UALL.o.w.e.d
Chicago, IL
City, State
www.uallowed.com

Publisher's Note: The Message Bible: *The Bible in Contemporary Language. Copyright ©2002 by Eugene H. Peterson*
Book Layout © 2017 BookDesignTemplates.com

The Power to Become/ Author. Mattie Stanford Johnson. -- 1st ed.
ISBN **13:978-0999012598**

Dedication

This book is dedicated to those who have struggled within themselves to be who they are. Those who felt as if they were never "enough." Know that you are enough and will always BE.

It is not about being someone else but rather Becoming who you already are.

Acknowledgement

God,

It is because of you I AM. Who am I that you are even mindful of me

Husband,

THANK YOU I love you so much. You are definitely a keeper. Many of our ups and downs helped me Become who I am today. We did this!

Children,

You all have tolerated the closed doors during this process. I LOVE YOU ALL to life. Watching each of you BE who you are is such a joy

Parents,

Because of your prayers and continuous love, I have BEcome the woman I am. I am beyond grateful for my upbringing. All four of you were the best thing that could ever have happened to me. Thank you for being examples I could look to in every aspect of life.

Siblings,

Each of us has different relationships and I am honored to have each of you in my life. Greatness is our portion. You all were with me in various steps Lil Jo being there from my beginning, I appreciate you all

Contents

Introduction 1

The Blessing in Becoming....................................1

Increased By God 9

    What is your TRUTH?....................................11

    You Are Good...13

    Becoming Fruitful 16

Born Powerful...21

    The Start of My Journey 24

    The Becoming of the Warrior 27

    Finding the Power Within Your Bloodline....30

Enough...33

M.A.D. 42

    Killing the Voices 44

    Celebrate Your Life 46

Finished Product on the Way..............................47

Enjoying the Process 50
Adding Detail 52
The Secret to Living 54
End on Empty 58

Introduction

Throughout many of our lives we have been told to just do this or just do that---- Do, Do, Do. Almost making one wonder why we're called human beings and not human doings. However, amidst all the background noise, you hear a small voice telling you to just be yourself and smack dab in the middle of having this conversation you start to feel the anxiety of all the things you felt you needed to DO instead of just BEing. Feelings of uncertainty, inadequacy and complacency all overwhelm you. You feel stuck. You feel like you can never add up.

The Power to BECOME will help eliminate EVERYTHING you feel and think, that is contrary to what the creator placed in side of you. You possess an unlimited power to become. You were born with everything you need to become who you were created to be. In this book, our goal is to reach the untapped intelligence, and leave no room for wasted potential.

For those of us who are looking for a deeper connectedness with ourselves this book will be of great value. Let us begin the journey to becoming who we were created to be. Information comes to our mind through our senses, and if our mind is not settled that information can become distorted. Inner turmoil and the conditioning of the past must be suspended so when we look with our eyes we don't fail to see, when we use our ears we don't fail to listen, and when we touch we don't do so, without feeling. We must come to a place where the simplest experiences and the use of our senses will bring us to a place of child likeness. When I speak of this child likeness, I speak of the time before conditioning and excessive sensory stimulation. The time when the absolute reality of who you will become is so vast and infinite that all the labels, words, systems, and thoughts put together cannot comprehend even a portion of who you truly are. For instance, if you are a mother your child will speak of you from that perspective whereas your friend, husband, parent, or neighbor all have different perceptions of you. Although all these perspectives and perceptions make your journey feel a million miles away from who you truly are; remember each journey starts with the first step.

Chapter 1

The Blessing in Becoming

Genesis 1:27(MSG)," God spoke: "Let us make human **BE**ings in our image, make them <u>reflecting</u> our nature."

Where does this power to become begin? The book of Genesis tells the story of creation, and how God decided to make human "BE"ings making them in a godlike image. God's very words were used to speak and bring forth our existence including the quality of our being. No matter how we came forth, our existence did not come for naught, but for the image of a true God to be reflected (manifest) and revealed on the earth.

The power to become begins with the reflection of God. Reflection is transformative and although there may have been times of feebleness, your life continues to experience conversion.

You were created to enjoy the bliss of heaven. Your thought of this possibility may be as mine that if I was created to enjoy the bliss of heaven, then why have I experienced nothing but hell here on earth? What would make me believe that now all of a sudden, I am supposed to have this power to become anything other than what I already am? If you are graced to read this book which was written by a prophet called by God, then know that God is allowing your very situation to be shifted and changed this very moment. The strength to believe is being imparted in you to walk through the journey of becoming who YOU, yes YOU were created to become.

THE POWER TO BECOME

Have you ever looked up the definition of become? Many times, we feel like knowing the definition of some words is common sense, so we never truly define them. We feel like we already know the meaning. Let me entertain you by playing words with friends. I have this very cool app on my phone and when I read or hear a word I'm not familiar with I go to the Advanced English Dictionary and Thesaurus. It indeed is a life saver, especially if you're not a word guru.

> ***Become (verb) means:***
>
> *Become, go, get enter or assume a certain state or condition*

Ok I'm getting excited already. The dictionary goes on to tell me to also see the words:

> *Progress, come on, come along, advance, get on, get along, shape up, get over,*

subdue, surmount, master, gain, win, pull ahead, make headway, gain ground.

Whew…… The book of Genesis tells the story of how God created the world; and used the words, "Let there Be." God wants us to become. Let's break this down and process what it means to become.

I am to progress in the dreams and visions that will later be revealed to me, come to a place that I may feel is too high for me, and come along with the guidance that will be provided to me throughout my life. I am also to advance in everything I am placed in, get on those rides I may be afraid to ride, get along with my family although I know down the road there will be some type of betrayal yet and still God decided those where the people I was going to share blood with and who are important to my development, shape up after knowing I was going to take a sabbatical in life longer than I should have; subdue anything that exalts itself against you and the belief that you choose me despite me; surmount all the naysayers that don't believe I was born to reach the highest point of what you called me to be; master my emotions; gain knowledge about who God is because in knowing him I will never ever doubt me; know that despite of everything that happens to me good, bad, and ugly, I will always WIN; pull ahead of distractions; make headway for all the blessings God has and will bestow upon me throughout my life and my children's, children's, children's lives; and gain ground even after the tremendous amount of heartbreak that I would suffer throughout my life. WOW!!! Your becoming is powerful. I need you to know that what becomes has duration. What God has called you to become is continuance, without interruption. You were blessed from the beginning to BE.

Since we were blessed from the beginning to BE, where does our perception of self-come from? Who told you who you were? Your perception of yourself must be clear so that you can appear as you are, "infinite," made in Gods image. You have infinite abilities being made in the image of God. When we speak of God, we say he is infinite. Yes! So, that means there is an innumerable amount of abilities on the inside of you. It needs to be understood that when you were created you were already a total package.

Here is a great example; when you buy something big many times it arrives in many pieces and must be put together, yet everything needed is already there. It just takes some time to put them all together. Now, place yourself in this scenario. You came on this earth with everything you need to become (insert your name). The question is, how and where did all the distorted views come from? Have we attached pieces that do not belong to us? Or have we placed the wrong pieces in the wrong place? Have you started with the parts the instructions clearly told you to hold on until last? If you are putting together a kitchen table, do you use the legs of the kitchen chairs? I'm sure some kind of way you can make it fit. However, that table will have some deformities if all the other legs are standing a certain way and one leg is shorter that the rest.

Whose distorted voice are you hearing? For some reasons, the past few years my hearing has not been the same. I say huh a whole lot more now. My family and friends say I should probably get my ears checked. However, to myself I've secretly asked God what would it be like if I did lose my hearing. While on the phone with one of my older mentors, she began telling me how she had just gotten a hearing aid. So me being the researcher that I am, guess what I did, I immediately started looking up hearing aids. There were 3 guidelines that should always be followed by the dispenser. The first was to restore audibility so that the amplified sound is above the user's threshold. The second thing was to limit the output so that the amplified signal does not exceed the user's discomfort level, and third, to do no harm so that the amplified signal is not unintentionally or undesirably altered by the hearing aid. I know you may be asking what does this have to do with anything Mrs. Mattie?

Well, I will go straight to the third guideline, do no harm. This guideline reveals the importance of hearing with no alteration of the signal other than that which the fitter (me) intends. In other words, something that is meant to assist me should not distort the desired sound. When I asked the question about distorted voices is it because of something you added thinking it would assist you or is it the cause of nothing sounding clear? Who and what have come into your life and distorted your mind?

When God created our minds, He created it with infinite potential. The average person's mind, not talking about people we consider geniuses, but the average brain contains approximately 100 billion nerve cells or neurons. Each neuron has connections. So, do you think that when it comes to thinking about ourselves, that we are to think small? No, we are to have limitless thoughts about who we will BEcome because sure enough there is a blessing in it and it increases us.

Take time to answer:

THE POWER TO BECOME

Am I thinking too small?

Whose voice have I been listening to?

Do the people around me have my best interest in mind?

Chapter 2

Increased By God

The definition of increase can be summed up in two phrases, "to become great" or "to add to." BEcoming greater, adding to what we already have and advancing, are all components of increase. It is not that increase does not occur in our BEcoming, yet it is our perception of increase that often causes us to falter. In our journey to become, increase comes through a commitment to the truth (seeing reality as it is), and not wanting more than is needed (If we waste not, we will want not.) How does me committing to the truth bring increase to me?

Here's a perfect example while counseling a young lady; she complained about how her family was never there for her and how they did not care for her. Well that was her truth. However, the reality was that she never allowed them to be there for her because she wanted to be superwoman to everyone; because this reaffirmed her sense of worth. As long as she felt needed, she felt important. She didn't realize she was placing herself in a position that would leave her with a void.

Discovering the truth about ourselves can be rather humbling, but it allows us to enter a place of consciousness about ourselves that will hopefully lead to self-mastery. Developed consciousness cultivates virtue. Virtue brings harmony and functioning of life. The development of one's self brings increase because it allows you to open up to areas you may have been closed off to. Development has the same root word as envelope— "De-enveloping" or opening up. While opening up to what is needed, you can't help but realize what is not needed. Increase again is attached to you because you place yourself in a position to not want more than needed.

Take time to answer:

Name something you are holding on to that is not needed?

What is your TRUTH?

It is said that, 95% of the beliefs we have stored in our minds are nothing but lies. We suffer repeatedly because we choose to continuously believe the lies. This is a grave injustice. We are blinded by the truth because of the false beliefs in our mind. Many times, our truth sounds like thousands of people talking at the same time with no one getting an understanding. Is your truth putting you in a mental prison and making you pay over and over for the same decisions you've made in the past?

You surrender to beliefs by agreement. As soon as you agree, it became your truth. What you consider to be a truth in one state of being, can be a lie in another. Many people say they fear death but the truth of the matter is that it is opposite that they fear life---living. Truth is a fact that has been verified. The things that you considered true because of what someone else told you or what you fear; if it has not been verified…. IT IS NOT TRUE.

Where are you getting your verifications from? Who is doing your fact checking? Are they biasing toward you? Do they envy you? As the old saints say, "Whose report will you believe?" I would rather check with my manufacturer, the one who created me and knew exactly why he made me and who I was to BE. If you don't know anything else, be aware that everything that GOD made was good.

> ***Take time to answer:***
>
> *What am I holding on to as truth even though it may be a lie?*
>
> *Do I have something or someone placing me in a mental prison?*
>
> *Is the person I allow to do my fact checking reliable?*

You Are Good

After God created everything, he sat back and said, "It is Good." You are part of that which he called good, we just struggle to see it for whatever reason. When we look at nature, our body, or even a seed, none of these things struggle to just BE. A seed doesn't struggle to become a tree, it simply unfolds in grace. The tree does not keep asking itself. "Am I a good tree?" Why should you get stuck on what your natural eye sees anyway, most of it is just an illusion?

Let's look at our natural body for instance. When we look in the mirror we don't see ALL that has taken place over time. The body you have now, not just talking about weight gain or loss, but only 2% of all atoms in our bodies are retained meaning 98% is GONE. We acquire a new liver in 6 months' time, new skin about once a month, and a new stomach lining every 5 days. Thank God, considering how some of us eat, for a new skeletal that constantly replaces itself. So just because you don't see change or think things are good, does not mean it has not occurred. You are good. Free yourself from the noise that tells you otherwise. Take time to be silent and just BE. Solitude enables intimacy with oneself. This time helps to take off labels that you and others have placed on you. Have you ever noticed what happens when asked, who are you? Most people respond with their job title first. Not realizing their identity but their industry. If you are not aware of who you are you will get stuck in what you do. But, what if that job was eliminated, then who would you be? If we were stripped of everything we have and know to be true, who would we be? I have gotten to the point where I just say I'm good.

> ***Take time to answer:***
>
> *Who am I?*
>
> *What is the truth about me beyond the noise?*
>
> *When was the last time I felt good?*

Becoming Fruitful

Genesis 1:28 (KJV), "*And God **blessed** them, and God said unto them, BE **fruitful**, and **multiply**, and **replenish** the earth, and **subdue** it: and have **dominion over** the fish of the sea, and over the fowl of the air, and over every living thing that moveth upon the earth.*"

Once God created us, He let us know what was required of us. Even in God giving requirements, He gives a blessing. Many look at God as saying to be fruitful, as if it was a command, however it was a blessing. I hear someone asking, how does God expect me to be fruitful when he knows I am barren? Excellent question. The fact that God declared fruitfulness as a blessing, means that He is the one who fulfills it. So, for us to feel it will never be accomplished by our own doing is incorrect. When someone gives (blesses) you with something, you must determine your part in the blessing? To receive. Is it really that simple?

THE POWER TO BECOME

After counseling several youth and young adults I have heard many say, "Lack is all they have ever seen in their families." According to them, they felt barren and fruitless. Fruitful means productive or conducive to producing in abundance, fertile, prolific.

We are like a seed with an unrealized potential of a tree: the tree is hidden in the very being of the seed—Only realized once the seed BECOMES the tree

Before you learned to do anything, and before anyone taught you, God blessed you to produce. God will not ask us to produce anything that is not already on the inside of us. It is in Him that we become ANYTHING. Reading Genesis 1:28 helped me to see God in a bigger light. The fact that He made man on his own accord shows that He didn't need man to be fruitful and have kids just to populate the earth. God very well could have done that himself. However, God blessing us to be fruitful gave us an ability to do whatever

He placed on the inside of us to do. The main thing in being fruitful in what he called you to do is leaving the weight of responsibility(ability) with him (GOD). The answer to the question how do we become fruitful, is rather simple. Produce. Know and believe. God has not set up your ability to produce contingent upon you, but rather contingent upon himself. He has set it up that instead of depending on your abilities, he wants you to trust him to produce in your life what pleases Him.

> ***Take time to answer:***
>
> *When talent, skill, or interest has God placed inside of you?*
>
> *When was the last time you believed God for anything or have you taken everything upon yourself to complete?*

Chapter 3

Born Powerful

Do you know what it took for you to arrive? Your birth was powerful. You may ask how do I know? Well, the simple fact that you even exist tells me so. Let's start with your conception. You won the biggest race you will ever run in your life. Remember how I told you that you were the star of the show. There was actually a cast of millions going for your spot. This race was not easy. There were many twists and plots you needed to get through even in the reproduction tract. You could have gotten lost on your way to fertilization but there was a power and grace upon you to get you where you needed to be before unfound dangers appeared. This all may sound like too much, but I need to break down just how powerful you are. So, you were released. And while some people feel as if their father has done nothing for them, let this bit of information heal you. Once he released, there was a portion of semen that was liquid which provided you with nourishment and fortified you for your journey. Come on let's give the dad's some credit. That was a major part of your coming into existence. If you didn't have that to get you where you needed to get in the time needed to get there, the vagina would have quickly destroyed every other cell.

You needed to get to a more welcoming environment, which was your mother's cervical canal; anything before this was hostile. This place transported you to a stream where you still did not fully exist. You spent an hour going through a change that was biochemical. You had to pick up speed and get into the uterus and fallopian tubes to find a target. Now mind you timing is important. So, don't ever again say "you can never be on time," your timing was perfect. If you had arrived too early, there would be a risk of dying before the egg showed up. If you were too late, the egg would have left. But hey, you made it to where you needed to be and when you needed to be there. However, there was STILL work to do. I pray this is not the hardest work you have done in your life. Anyway, there was a hard-outer layer of the egg, and yes at this point there are others still in the race competing. You thought it was just you at this point, NO there were hundreds surrounding your egg, battling away to be the one to finish. This was where you fought to release your genetic contribution. You had the power to become what you needed to be in that moment. You were powerful and not powerless in this mission. Your success of penetrating the egg immediately underwent a reaction that was chemical and prevented all those other folks who tried from coming into your spotlight.

Just like in your mother's womb, your survival was a pure miracle. So, do you actually think that you made it through all of that, just to become a waste of life. Not so. You may have gone through many things, but survived. You had what it took to make it here. You have enough in you, even though you are still growing. You have enough to continue where you were to where you are.

The Start of My Journey

Looking back on my childhood and remembering my younger day, there is one day that always comes to mind. My older brother and I sharing a room with a big dumb clown on the wall. Waking up Lil Jo would ask me where you wanted to go and I have no clue why I would scream "to hell." I would laugh and my brother would quickly tell me that I shouldn't say that. Why do I remember this so vividly? Why this memory out of so many? Why did that even come out of my mouth while growing up a PK (preacher's kid). Being born and raised in the church, where did that come from?

I believe at the age of 5, I wanted to say something to shock others. Although the enemy of my soul would use that very memory to taunt me and say that would surely be my future. As I write this book, for the first time I realize that was just a reminder that I will always have the words that will shock someone. The words that will make someone think beyond the place or the question they are pondering. I would always have the ability to allow people to see me passed the labels placed on me: PK, black girl, rebellious one, untamed, rule breaker. I would be the one to journey through life without limits and limitation even if it made others uncomfortable. I would become unapologetic in my truth and would be the one to carve out my own path and inspire others by uprooting their inhibitions. Looking over my life I may not have literally went to hell, but I have been there and back many times with mental bondage, self-sabotage, sickness and more. However, the moral of the story is, "I ALWAYS CAME BACK." I am the definition of the comeback kid on a journey to BEcoming who I was destined to be before hell thought it had me. My journey is not yours, though some of my story may also be the story of someone that is reading this. I am here to let you know that the power to become was placed inside of you right as your little limbs were growing in your mother's womb. You were born with a power and that power is YOU. The power we all have is that NO ONE else can be who we are. Isn't that powerful? That is a place of uniqueness. That is a place of authenticity. There is no competition there. There is only one winner in your story.

Yes! There are other characters but the main character, the one who owns the show, the one who can never be replaced, the one who will win at the end, is YOU, yes you. There is not a person in this world, even if you have the exact same name, that will become YOU. With this being said, there are some that are reading and saying, I don't want to be me. I am not enough. Being me is too hard. Becoming something other than the failure I am being; is too great. But I am a living witness and it's not just cliché, if you are breathing, if you are alive, there is still time to become your purpose. Remember you were already born with the power. You just have to tap into your power not your pain. Do not finalize your future with your present state. There is so much more to this story. We denounce the lies that things will never change. We denounce the guilt of past mistakes. We denounce fear of being great and we denounce anything that tells us there is no purpose for our lives. There is a power to become that we all were born with that allows us to live the "I AM" life. The life that has the ability to transform us to whatever we need to be in the moment we need to be it.

We embrace this power that is pushing us past mediocrity, past hurt and pains of the past, past insecurities, past failures, past loss of influential love ones, and past word curses that proclaim we will never mount to anything, past discouragement, and past uncertainties. We embrace self-love, the will to move forward, and the strength to try one more time. The POWER we were born with is being released to BECOME.

MATTIE STANFORD JOHNSON

The Becoming of the Warrior

Growing up as a child I was always engaged in warfare. I never realized it was because I was warrior. Even my name Mattie, means "Mighty in Battle." Growing up I hated my name because it seemed that everyone would say that it was their grandma's name. Who wanted an old folks name? I would complain about my name and both of my parents would blame one another for the reason my name was Mattie. My dad said, "Your mom wanted you named after her." Many of my cousins still call me Little Mattie. My mom says, "I wanted to name you Asia, that was your daddy who named you." However, once I learned the meaning of my name, it felt as if my purpose was revealed to me and the understanding for so many struggles was answered.

I was always a fighter and hated injustice done to anyone. I would take on many battles that weren't necessarily my own. I even named my first-born Justice. I never liked to see people struggle especially at the hands of others. Who knew the power to become this warrior started with my name? Every time I was called "Mattie," I was being called "Mighty." Once I realized that I was to be great in battle, I had a new perspective on what battles I would fight. It's not that I wouldn't fight any that were not my own, but I would fight with a greater passion and purpose. Like I stated earlier, there was power already inside of me.

The power of the warrior is still in the process of becoming. What does your name mean? Knowing this is important not just so you can put all your experiences and attributes together to build an image in your mind, but also to help us build a connection. For example, many cultures attach extreme importance to a baby's naming because in some way they feel the name will give the child some sort of guidance. Find out what your name means, there just may be a powerful message waiting for you.

Whether we believe it or not, many of our names shaped our self-esteem and identity. I am one who really does not care for nicknames, ask my son Justice. He reduced his wonderful wholesome name down to J-Dot. Huh? What's a J-Dot? Every time I heard a friend call him that I cringed. One day I asked him to look up the definition of dot. He came back with a definition, a small spot, speck. Yes, I was very hard and extra as my children put it. So, you are asking everyone to call you a speck, huh? He simply said, "Ma, I get it."

Names have weight. Your name is how you market yourself. It's your brand for the rest of your life. There have been studies that have shown that names set up certain expectations and can influence people who place weight on first impressions. The name you create for yourself will influence perceptions, even though those perceptions will fade away as the real person and their qualities appear.

Take time to answer:

What will people know about you?

What is the meaning of your name?

Will your name leave a legacy?

Finding the Power Within Your Bloodline

I found power while looking over my life and going through my family bloodline. Often times when you feel weak or frail and like you are a failure, take yourself back through how you arrived at that point. There is so much power, even for my Debbie downers that feel like not only are they a loser, but their whole family is too. I can tell you that this is so far from the truth as evidenced by this one statement that, "We survived because our ancestors refused to die." Although we may be surrounded by those that choose not to live up to the powerful bloodline that exists does not mean that someone from your line won't.

You, yes you, the one who is reading this very passage. You have the power to redeem your bloodline. For you to be here today, means there were generations after generations of survivors. Someone's entire bloodline had been wiped out, however, not yours because you are here. There is power that lies within your lineage. There was a divine purpose for why you were born in the family you were born in. And just as there are certain demons that try to take over a family, there are also blessings. You may be thinking "Oh you don't know my family." I don't know your family, but I know you picked up a book titled "The Power to Become," meaning you know you are to become someone powerful. What I am saying is not alternative facts either, as we have been hearing about in our news outlets.

You may be looking at your outer appearance and your present situation and saying there is no power here, but please believe me when I say, there is power in the blood to become the champion you were sent here to become. Have you ever looked at someone else and compared yourself, you say things like, they have good hair or her voice is so heavenly, or his intelligence is superior to mine? Let me explain to you that looking at someone from the outside does not tell what type of blood is flowing through them.

I know we are not animals, but it does not suggest that they are thoroughbreds. Even if you have identical twins, the difference is in the blood. I use the bloodline analogy to explain what is inside of you, because just like we can't live without the blood on the inside of us, it is the same with your purpose. Your life is depending on what is inside of you. Just as our blood delivers nutrients and oxygen to cells, our purpose for becoming is to be deliverers of our stories. We will deliver purpose to many, and give what is necessary for them to function in their daily lives. We will be the breath of fresh air needed at someone's lowest point. Just as blood transports waste from the cells, we too will be the vessel God uses to transport others from here to there. Other people will be relieved from waste places because you chose to BEcome who you were created to be. Your life will be blessed even the more in your becoming.

Chapter 4

Enough

Have you ever been asked the question, "What advice would you give your younger self?" I always answer that question whenever asked with, "You are enough!" There were so many times where growing up, although I wasn't a bad kid, I felt like being who I was, just was not enough. I felt like a failure although I always had good grades. I felt mediocre in high school although I graduated with honors and was the Student Council President. Although things on the outside appeared good and great to others, I struggled with thoughts in my head that always said, YOU ARE NOT ENOUGH.

To be totally honest as I write this book that you are reading, thoughts have tried to overtake me and tell me that I don't have enough to say to write a book. If you are reading this book guess what, I HAD WHAT IT TOOK to complete the book. I was born with it. Later in this book I talk about killing the voices that try to drown out the truth about you. One of the sayings that is out now, "Let me be GREAT." This is what I use to drown out those negative thoughts of comparison. As I stated earlier, competition is limited because we only compete with the person we were yesterday.

While typing this: I have won because I was supposed to write yesterday and I did not. I played games on my phone; then went out to eat with a friend and knew I needed to write, so already today I beat who I was yesterday. I'll just use the saying, "If you want to do something big, you have to do something little every day." What little do you want to work on today? It can be something as simple as getting out of the bed, because that may have been a struggle yesterday. I know because I've been there before as well. Maybe the little thing to do today is to register for one class. Don't try to think about a daunting degree just register for one class.

Currently as I write this book, I am preparing to write my dissertation for my doctoral program. Now everyone says, "Wow, you must really be smart to accomplish something like that," and I simply say, "No, not really, I just didn't quit." I passed one class at a time. There are many levels to greatness. However, each level takes several steps and the only way to take several steps is to start with one. If you know I am speaking to you in this chapter let's take a few small steps. Often, we never give credit to the very small steps we take which are necessary for overall change.

First step—embark on a journey of self-discovery. The feeling of not being enough simply comes from not knowing who you truly are. We will challenge ourselves for the next 30 days to write one thing we love about ourselves. I will give you a simple example, I love my nose. It took me a while to get to this place because growing up I was called Miss Piggy. I had a rather large nose but now I believe I have grown into it rather nicely. However, it bothered me that I was always called big nose and I hated it. Once I got to high school it grew worse because a dark line went right across it as if it wasn't already big. No, it wasn't from glasses. I always tried to wear glasses but 20/20 was always my portion. So where did this line come from? I still don't know, but it disappeared years later. Yes, for years I had a line across my big nose and I never found out where it came from, work with me.

Anyhow I started to realize the power in the senses of this big nose that I had. I mean, I could smell things others could barely smell. If you want to go deeper, my nose gave me a greater ability to process air that I breathed before it entered my lungs. Ok, so does yours, but I had to dig deep to learn to appreciate and love things about me that I felt like I hated. So back to our first step, we will write one thing we love about ourselves. Now if you feel like that's easy I love noting about me, you're still not out of the challenge, you will write about every limb and organ of the body till you get to 30 and study it because we will get to a point where we will love ourselves. The deeper you explore yourself, the greater power comes with your being. Once you start digging deeper and acknowledging your "enoughness," you can move on to the next step.

The second step--- Letting Go. Alan Watts a philosopher, writer, and speaker wrote, "Waking up to who you are requires letting go of who you imagine yourself to be." This step is so important because the practice of letting go is used to support everything you have just accepted about yourself. Self-acceptance is a cornerstone of creating a full and happy life. However, this step may be the toughest of them all because as you begin to let things go, even things that may have been bad in your past, it will seem like your identity is being stripped away from you.

We come against depression that may try to step in at this point and make us feel as though we are nothing and that our life is now void. God, we ask that the person reading this is filled with peace and joy about their past, present, and future. Allow them to know and feel that what they are feeling is what is needed on their journey to become. Just like a caterpillar, allow them to realize that beauty is coming out of the ugly. Allow them to realize that just as they got through the race for life, there is a complete metamorphosis happening even now. God, we ask as we walk through this step of letting go that you continue to feed us glimpses of who we are to become.

For just like the larva stage of a caterpillar allow us to have an appetite for what is to come. As we eat only what is good for our growth, allow us to expand quickly. Now as I understand that the caterpillar exoskeleton (skin) does not stretch but shed, allow us to shed the layers of dysfunction that keeps us from functioning in our true calling. Allow us to shed skin that is callused to love because we feel like love has only brought us pain. Allow us to shed off any and everything that will stunt our growth. Just as the caterpillar has shed the outgrown skin, there is another stage of letting go called the Pupa stage. At this point we have reached full length and weight.

THE POWER TO BECOME

Now although you may still not see the beauty of where you are in this phase because of outside appearances and to some it looks as if you're just resting or doing completely nothing—inside there is action taking place. The change is rapid.

What God is doing for you right now is rapid. Old habits are changing even you haven't realized it yet. Transformation has come to your heart. This work may not have appeared from the outside yet but it's happening on the inside. You're now loving who you are and letting go of unforgiveness to yourself and others. Did you know that a caterpillar at this point has new body parts and that as they start to emerge, tissue, limbs and organs have all been changed by this time? I speak to your health right now, for your tissue, cells, limbs, and organs to line up to its rightful place. We need to be healthy and in letting go of bitterness and unforgiveness our health at this very hour is being restored. The last phase before the caterpillar becomes a butterfly, is the pumping of blood into the wings to get them working and flapping—then they fly. It usually takes the butterfly three to four hours to master flying, after which they find a mate to reproduce. Now in your last phase of letting go, it will take some pumping of blood, sweat, and tears to get things to work.

Once we get to a place where we have mastered emotions and self-love, we can help reproduce these actions in others. Now let me go back. They mastered flying in three to four hours. Why does it take us so long to master things? I believe if we live in the moments of our becoming and master those daily moments, we will master things just as the butterfly. I also believe because they let go of skin it gave them more mobility in their wings. They did not have to carry extra weight. Let us be like the butterfly and let things go so that we can fly off and reproduce in a generation that is waiting on those who have mastered areas they feel they are failing.

Our third step is to become the author of our own life. Step one puts you in a place of loving who you are; meaning you have new definitions of what it means to be successful, a great parent, or even what happiness is to you. Step two helped to let go of who you were not. In becoming the author of your own life, you now write your story. How is your story taking a turn for the better? You are no longer looking at someone's life and defining your own.

All the definitions that we have picked along the way are useless to where we are going. You have chosen to view your life from different lenses and your writing is not from a victim's standpoint but a victor. Your story defines you as one who defied all the odds despite the various circumstances. Becoming the author of your own life has made you take a stance on what/who you will allow to give meaning to your destiny. Becoming the author of your life has helped you resume the position of power that you were indeed born with. This position of power you continue to give yourself by authoring your life takes courage and authority. With you being the author of your life, you have the authority to change mistakes and failures into stepping stones.

Although we wish to get approval on these changes we are making from folks on the outside, the true authority and approval must come from within you. I read a statement that said, "Permission to be fully authentic is a self-given authority." So, while writing your own story understand that you have permission to be fully authentic, this way there will never be a story quite like yours. Their story may have many of the same setbacks, comebacks, or whatever, but none will ever be yours. Why? Because there will always be only one YOU.

The power of each of these steps is that the more you align with your whole self, the more the world rushes in to meet you where you are.

Chapter 5

M.A.D.

Make a decision. A full life is lived in the moments of decision. The decisions you make or refuse to make will determine the quality of your life. What decisions do you need to make in the coming days or weeks to become? The relationship that you are in, is it a strain, pain, or does it build you up? Decide to stay or decide to go…. But don't continue to just merely live. Extraordinary people decide.

Take time to answer:

What should you be M.A.D. about?

What is keeping you from deciding? Is it fear, lack of support, laziness, lack of motivation, or mediocrity? Decide to live out some of the dreams you let go of. Did you know that 80% of people do not live out their dreams? Does that mean that many are living out the dreams of 20 percent of people? Whose dream have you said was more important than yours? These questions are being asked because they need to be answered.

Life is more than just getting by. You must decide by making a statement. Your words are your power to create what you decided. I decided to live with peace of mind. I have decided I will be a nurturing mother. I decided I will accept that, "I AM GREAT." I decided I will finish this book so that you can read it. I decided I will become more accountable for my actions by taking responsibility. I decided I will not judge or blame myself. I decided I will believe in myself again. I decided I will hope again. I decided I will believe again. I decided I will love more. I decided I will give those who I allowed in my life 100% of me. I decided I will not walk in mediocrity. I decided I will save. I decided I will no longer lack. I decided to become disciplined. I decided to walk tall. I decided to think big. I decided to think bigger. I decided to trust in the Great "I AM." I decided I want to be loved to the fullest. I decided I will always be a giver. I decided I will kill the voices that are negative. I decided to DECIDE.

Killing the Voices

What are these constant voices in your head? We say people that walk around talking to themselves are crazy but really, we are the same way we just don't speak to the voices out loud. We have judges, prosecutors, tormentors, cheerleaders, bullies, pushovers, all judging and guiding our every move but because we are conditioned by these voices, our future will only become the past. This distorted view will never allow you to become.

Kill the voices. Learn to misidentify with a voice that is not promoting you to BECOME. Many of us suffer simply because the voices whisper desires we should have which cause us pain from not having. We must cut the bonds of desire. Most desires are for things that are external and overshadow becoming. These desires cause us to seek for fulfillment outside ourselves. We are gripped with the pain of non-fulfillment. Get out of the grip of this pain. Don't say I want to achieve this or that and get caught up in the continuous pain of not meeting your potential.

For one moment forget about the time and just live and BE. Close the gap of anxiety that try and BE. What are you doing now to become who you are called to be? Are you in the future somewhere waiting on some type of change to take place for you? You're in an anxiety gap. Your saying look! You got me all excited to become something now you are saying pause. NO, I am saying bridge the gap of anxiety. This anxiety comes when the voices overwhelm your being. Stop the voices and become aware of your thoughts and emotions. Step back and analyze what is happening around you. Right now, you have decided to take the once class and you're excited, you have done well. The voices now creep in and tell you, now you must finish the degree. KILL THE VOICES. Regroup and tell yourself, "I will be anxious for nothing." These thoughts, voices, and feelings will not control my being. You stop to celebrate your achievement of passing the one class and take action by signing up for the next class. That's it that's all. When people ask, "When are you going to finish that degree?" You calmly respond, "This class will be finished by whatever date." This stops the outer and inner turmoil and voices that tries to take on more than you should at that very moment. We know there is a finished product on the way, but today let me be great where I am.

Celebrate Your Life

There is a quote I remember reading, by Oprah Winfrey that stated, "The more you praise and celebrate your life, the more there is in life to celebrate." The power to become comes with the daily celebration of life. Find the simple joys to help remind you to slow down, celebrate life, and enjoy the moment. Once it is all said and done, your legacy will be tall, wide, and ever so deep. Expansion will be your portion in every area.

Chapter 6

Finished Product on the Way

Have you ever just sat back and looked at the pieces of your life? Or the time of many occurrences where you were totally baffled. How about asking why certain things had to happen? For a while that was me, until one day I started piecing things that happened together like a puzzle. When I was 16 years old, I used to go inside the prison down the street from my house and preach to those who were incarcerated. My burden was so great for those that had made past mistakes. I often wondered why at a young age was that my burden?

I loved delivering the message of hope, encouragement, and restoration. I loved seeing their smiles light up and hope reawakened within them. Suddenly that phase of my life was over. The passion, however, never died, just that assignment. I went on to become the kid who was this amazing preacher that many wanted their youth to hear. On various occasions, I was told who I should and should not be around. It seemed to others that my crowd was not suitable for the up and coming evangelist. I was one for underdog. Some of my leaders at the time would say, "It just don't look good. Why is this one or that one your friend?" This bothered me a great deal because in my eyes I was no better that the next person. We all lived by Grace. I felt like we all are one bad decision or mistake away from ruining our next opportunity if not mindful of our present decisions.

I believed with everything in me equality should be in everything and for everyone.

However, life did not prove to be so. Remember earlier how I told the story of fighting battles that weren't necessarily mine. It cost me in many ways. However, while writing today I realized that EVERYTHING was working in my favor, every piece that may not have fit in the puzzle then, fits now. Today I realized that my life story is beautiful. Things I did not understand are now understood. Those things that are not fully understood is okay because there is a different kind of joy in unfolding and unwrapping….

Do you remember loving to look at the Christmas tree or getting a gift that was wrapped? There was a joy you had in knowing that there was a gift but also a joy in unwrapping the gift. Don't let there be some bubble wrap in the packaging. Who enjoyed popping that stuff? Anyway, you wanted to get to the gift, but you enjoyed the moment of unwrapping it, that is how life is. I'm no longer anxious to get to the finished products my life will produce. I have learned and I am still learning to enjoy the process, to put detail to what is coming. Your life is a finished product if you rush to get to the end, what's next?

Enjoying the Process

Often time we don't enjoy life as it is because we have not directed our focus on living fully. It's like we are racing to get to the other end of the dash. You know your birthday dash and the date of death. As I stated in the chapter before, I am learning to enjoy the process. You may wonder what are some things I can do to enjoy the process. Learn to enjoy what it is you're currently doing. How does this help me enjoy my process? Think about one thing you do the most (eat, read, train, social media) it is likely that one thing is something that you enjoy, which is why you continue to do it. So, we must find the joy within our process. When we find this joy, it helps us to be thankful. It is easy to take the simplest things; --like walking, for granted. I remember right after graduating high I left one of my friend's house to get to my dad's church so I could take a nap only to lose my ability to walk. I woke up and was in excruciating pain. I had to be carried down the stairs by a couple of men, placed in a car and rushed to the hospital only for them to look at me as if I was crazy. Feeling had arrived back into my legs but I was in severe pain. The occurrence of pain came back a few days later and I couldn't walk. Again, I rushed to Cook County Hospital, one of the best hospitals to exist, only to be diagnosed with Sickle Cell Disease.

Really? So, I was born with a disease no one notices not even me till I was 17-years old. Looking back now and knowing what I know about this disease, I was blessed to get through elementary and high school without all those absences that would have occurred had I lost my strength to walk. I said all of this to say that I am learning to enjoy the process because although I may not understand everything, sometimes it just takes time to be revealed. God knew I didn't need another label "the sick kid," in high school.

When those painful instances would occur and my ability to walk were challenged once I recovered a feeling of gratitude overtook me. I was just happy to be able to walk. In going through the process of recovery of any type of

Dis-ease we must still thank God for the process because many times the things that were the hardest, made us the strongest. This reminds me of the process of a diamond and it's first method is high pressure.

Are you under high pressure right now? How is your process going? The process will teach one patience. Society with its smartphones, microwaves, email, and social media has created a people who crave instant gratification. This has also made people more frustrated and likely to give up easily when they don't get something quick enough. We must learn that the process is something to bring out the fullness of who we are becoming.

Adding Detail

What happens when you add detail to your story? The who, what, when, where, and why is answered. Every detail adds a special element to your celebration of Becoming. Even while looking at the most beautiful wedding or the grandest project, the success depends on the smallest components.

I know many use the phrase, "The devil is in the details." However, I beg to differ, because when I look at the solar system and the stars, or even the human body, I would have to say that God is the one that is into details. There is so much detail in the natural engineering of the human body. Our brain power alone is superior, not to mention the parts of us that we can't see. Our body is representing about 100 trillion or 100,000,000,000,000 cells that collectively form a human being. We are talking about details, right? Now just think each cell has its own task. If you want to continue to believe you lack power or greatness, just take time to study your body from the inside-out. Start with the cells, then cell structure, cell chemistry, tissues and on to organs and systems. Continue with the moving framework: hair, skeletal system, skull, backbone and ribs, limbs and girdles, hands and feet, bones in evolution, bone structure, growth and repair, joints, the muscular system, and skeletal muscles. Should we continue? The nervous system:

neurons, synapse, nerves, reflexes, and the cardiovascular system. I need you to get my point. There is power in the details of being—your life. You may not like anything about your physical body, but pay attention to the details. We as individuals will undergo continuous processes of mental and physical development and details of that is what makes our stories even more beautiful.

Chapter 7

The Secret to Living

There is a Tibetan Proverb that says the secret to living well and longer is to eat half, walk double, laugh triple and love without measure. Do you believe there is truth to this proverb? In our journey to become and utilize our power within, we must find what will make our life well and our living longer. My maternal grandmother is currently 95-years young. I wish I could show you a picture of her, you would not believe it. If the music of James Brown is on she will out dance any of her grandchildren, and just recently we were amazed at how well she bowled.

Yes, I'm talking about a 95-years old woman. Often, I listen to her tell her stories in complete amazement of how well she lives. Now of course she does not admit to doing everything right but from where I'm looking her life is perfect. This is exactly how our lives will be. Someone, somewhere will admire your story. They will say, "Wow! You are perfect."

I asked my grandma what her secret to living was and she would always smile and say, "I just lived." So from watching my grandma as a child and now being an adult with children of my own I can honestly say I have never seen her my grandmother down. Does that mean she never had moments that may have made her sad? No! However, she always chose to keep a smile on her face. She has a beautiful smile. I believe that is one of the things I inherited from her. The other thing grandma does is walk. So maybe that proverb mentioned earlier may have some truth to it. My grandma has yet to drive. She loves to walk. She gets out and stretches her legs daily.

She is extremely active. At the age of 95 she still lives alone and my mom often worries about her; and of course, because she still only has a land line phone to contact her. I politely tell my mom, "Momma, she out." Sure, enough she was out. She either walked to the store to get her famous scratch offs, caught a bus to the race track to bid on the horses, or went right on to the casino to win big. The secret to her living well and longer is that she does what she enjoys. Remember we mentioned that too? I am sure throughout her life people told her she needed to stop wasting her money on those scratch offs, or what I used to hear my momma say, "You done bought one of those horses, as long as you been going to the race-track." But she continued to do what she enjoyed. Hey! It works for her. That is what I am talking about. She enjoys being who she is, and doing what she does. She didn't make it this far by listening to the naysayers, she always just wanted to live.

Granma of course has several stories that she shares; like when she was little and picked cotton in the cotton fields and was pretty good at it as she says, but was too small to carry her own bag, or stories of her being a swing dancer. Out of all her stories I am amazed at how she loves life. My great grandmother, which was her mom, died when she was just two years of age and her dad died when she was five. Can you imagine? Surviving without those who were placed here to help shape and steer you. Oh, did I mention she was also a twin but the only one that survived.

Another one of grandma's secrets to living long and well was her prayer every night to live another day. With her parents dying so early in life, her fervent prayer to God was for her to live long enough to see her children grown. Well, God is a God that honors fervent prayers because not only is she alive to see her children become adults she has also seen her grandchildren become adults while also witnessing her great-grandchildren of the verge of adulthood. So, prayer is a secret to living long and well on your journey to becoming. The thing about this that gets me kind of choked up with emotion is that she knew what she wanted her future to be like. She made it simple and yet it is something that many have yet to aspire to. Although she lives for today she speaks to her future. If you were to call her right now and ask her how she is doing, she will would reply, "I'm 100." I have no doubt in my mind this lady will see the 100 mark if she chooses.

End on Empty

End knowing your story was complete and that you emptied out everything that was on the inside of you for the world to see and for your legacy to continue. End on empty means your story was so powerful that everyone wanted to hear it. Everyone wanted a taste, and everyone became full. You poured out. Ending on Empty is not a bad thing. Ending on empty robs the richest place on this earth, the grave yard.

Do not allow the grave to take anything from you. It has taken many others dreams, passions and exist without being empty. Some still had more to give, and more to be. They still had a voice to sing. They still had just one more dance. Many had one more great speech like Martin Luther King's "I Had a Dream Speech." Some died still full like Moses with vision still in his eyes.

When it is all over for me I want to know that I have given all that I could give. I want to know that the power I was born with was utilized to become. I want to know that I BECAME. I left a legacy of wealth, knowledge, peace, wisdom, and purpose for my children's, children's children to carry on. I became who I was created to be. I emptied out and BECAME.

MATTIE STANFORD JOHNSON

Mattie Stanford Johnson M.Ed. is wife to Brent D. Johnson Sr. and mother to 10 children. She is the founder of UALL.o.w.e.d. and Co-founder of Back to the Basic Organizations. Mattie S. Johnson is a multi-gifted author, motivational speaker and life coach. She cares passionately about seeing EVERYONE live a life on purpose particularly those that have been counted out. Mattie's life work consists of working with at-risk youth, those incarcerated, and returning citizens. In deciding to live by choice and not by chance Mattie S. Johnson has inspired others to move to a higher ground in an uplifting way. She is known as a deliver, a modern-day Harriet leading many from various grips of oppression.

www.ingramcontent.com/pod-product-compliance
Lightning Source LLC
LaVergne TN
LVHW051510070426
835507LV00022B/3033